**Edition Schott**

## Alvin Singleton

b.1940

# Between Sisters

for Soprano, Alto Flute, Vibraphone, and Piano

**ED 30040**
ISMN 979-0-60001-062-2

www.schott-music.com

Mainz · London · Madrid · New York · Paris · Prague · Tokyo · Toronto

# Foreword

*Between Sisters* (1990) is a musical setting of *The House Slave*, a poem by former U.S. Poet Laureate and Pulitzer Prize winner Rita Dove, and is scored for soprano, alto flute, vibraphone, and piano. Singleton here captures the just-awakening house slave woman's total powerlessness in the face of her field slave sister's and indeed all field slaves' hopelessly brutalized circumstances.  Silence, sometimes as if listening for something and at other times seeming to dramatize a lack of answers, is a major player in the sonic palette of this polytonally blue work.  Gone are the flute's typically florid lyricism and the piano's dexterity and power; and gone are the vibraphone's customary sexiness and quicksilver runs.  Instead both the soprano vocalist and the instruments moan and peep out their pitches and unresolvable harmonic consequences until suddenly at one heart-wrenching penultimate passage the singer shouts forth the desperate words "'oh, pray,' she cries," "'oh, pray.'" Then quiet again as the vibraphone turns to the fragile steady beating of muffled quarter notes (called "dead strokes") over held tones in the other instruments as the soprano sings "and as the fields unfold to whiteness, and they spill like bees among the fat flowers..." as if the clock that never stops beats hopelessly on for the slave.  All then closes softly in its powerful powerlessness.

Carman Moore

## The House Slave

The first horn lifts its arm over the dew-lit grass
and in the slave quarters there is a rustling —
children are bundled into aprons, cornbread

and water gourds grabbed, a salt pork breakfast taken.
I watch them driven into the vague before-dawn
while their mistress sleeps like an ivory toothpick

and Massa dreams of asses, rum and slave funk.
I cannot fall asleep again.  At the second horn,
the whip curls across the backs of the laggards —

sometimes my sister's voice, unmistaken, among them.
"Oh! Pray," she cries. "Oh!  pray!"  Those days
I lie on my cot, shivering in the early heat,

and as the fields unfold to whiteness,
and they spill like bees among the fat flowers,
I weep.  It is not yet daylight.

*Between Sisters* was commissioned by ensemble Thamyris with the support of Spelman College and the City of Atlanta Mayor's Fellowship in the Arts (Andrew Young, Mayor ).  The work is dedicated to former Spelman College president Johnnetta B. Cole

**World Premiere:**

October 23, 1990
Spelman College
Atlanta, Georgia


**Thamyris**

Cheryl-Boyd-Waddell, soprano
Paul Brittan, alto flute
Peggy Benkeser, vibraphone
Laura Gordy, piano

# Between Sisters

Rita Dove

Alvin Singleton (1990)

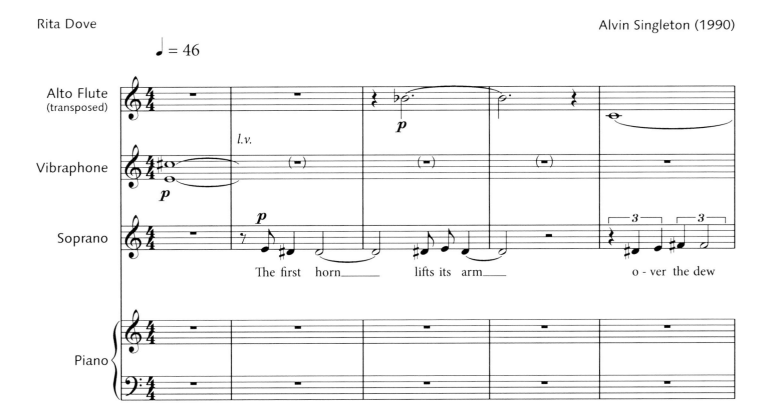

The first horn____ lifts its arm____ o - ver the dew

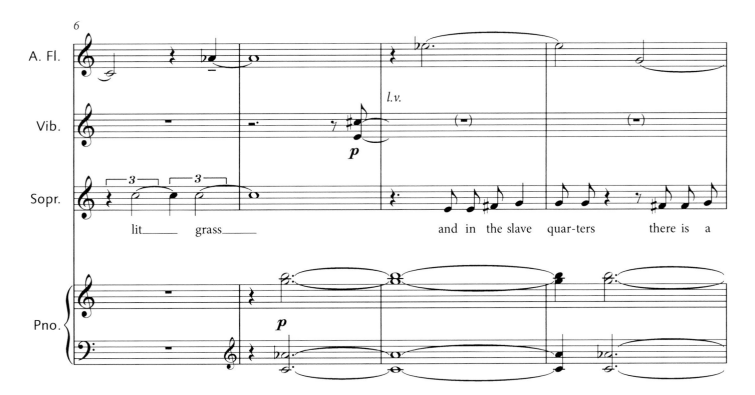

lit____ grass____ and in the slave quar-ters there is a

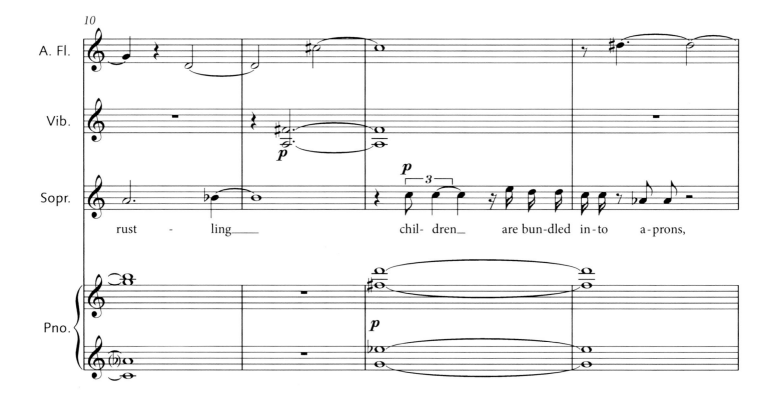

rust - ling___ chil- dren__ are bun-dled in-to a-prons,

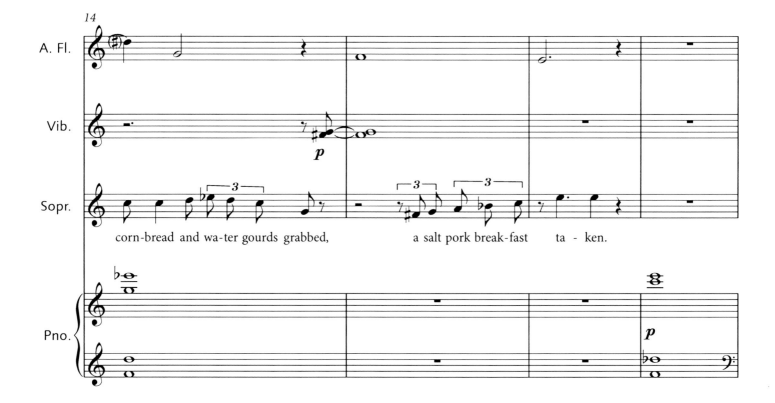

corn-bread and wa-ter gourds grabbed, a salt pork break-fast ta - ken.

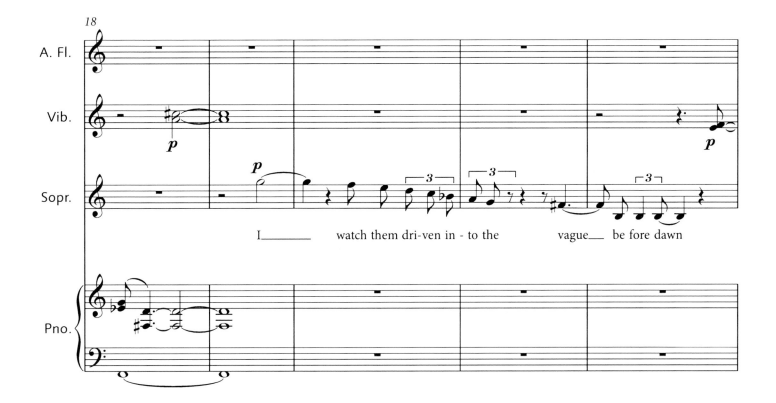

I_____ watch them dri-ven in - to the vague___ be fore dawn

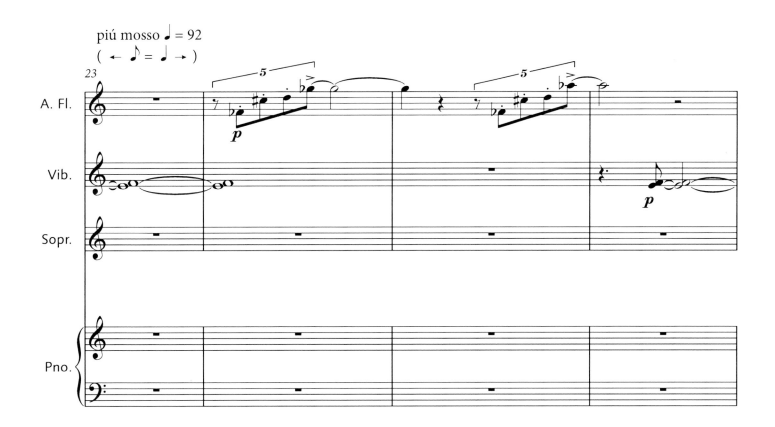

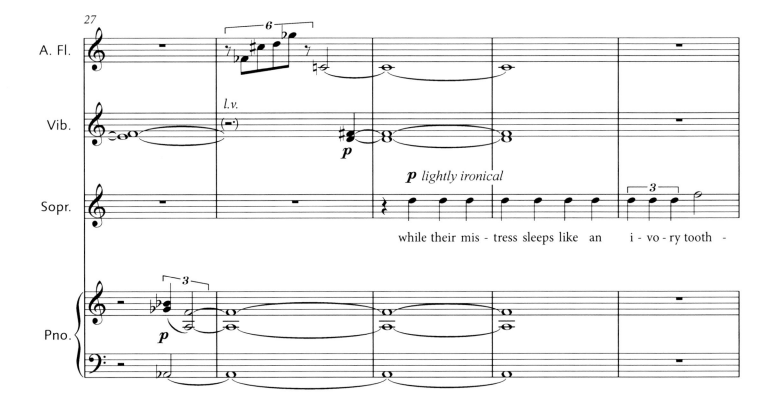

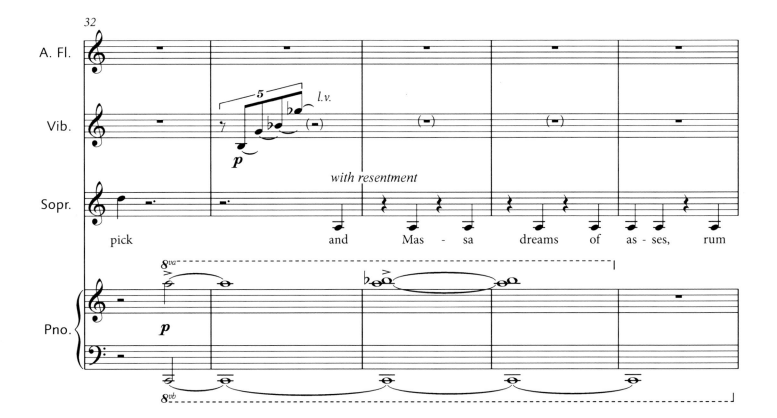

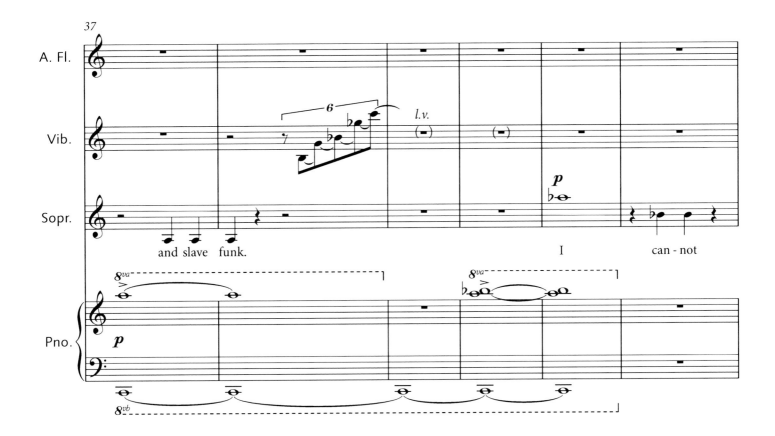

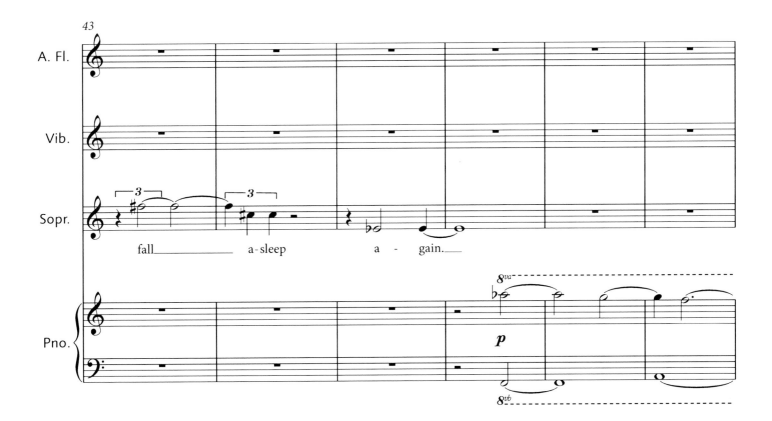

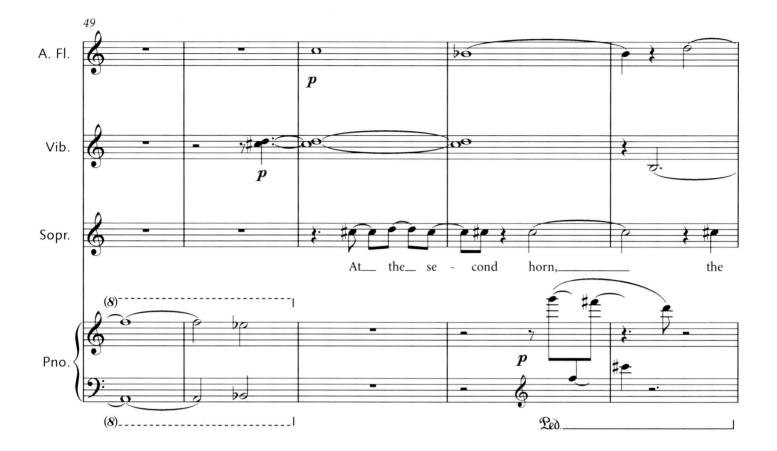

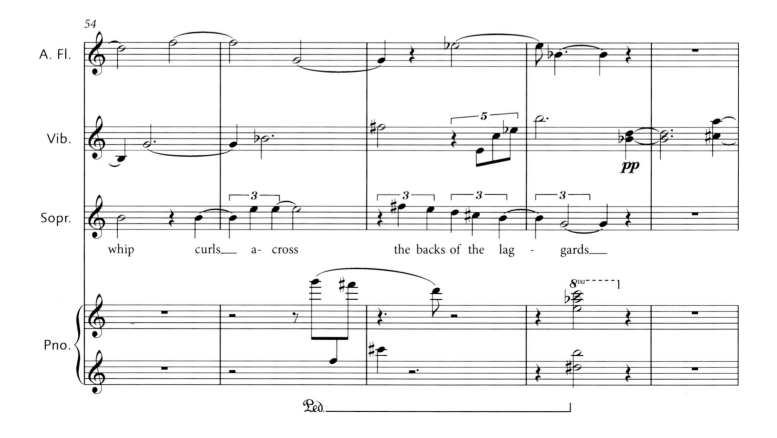

**Edition Schott**

**Alvin Singleton**

b.1940

# Between Sisters

for Soprano, Alto Flute, Vibraphone, and Piano

**ED 30040**
ISMN 979-0-60001-062-2

**Alto Flute Part**

www.schott-music.com

**SCHOTT**

Mainz · London · Madrid · New York · Paris · Prague · Tokyo · Toronto
© 2010 SCHOTT MUSIC CORPORATION, New York · Printed in USA

Alto Flute

# Between Sisters

Rita Dove

Alvin Singleton (1990)

Alto Flute

**Edition Schott**

Alvin Singleton

b.1940

# Between Sisters

for Soprano, Alto Flute, Vibraphone, and Piano

**ED 30040**
ISMN 979-0-60001-062-2

**Vibraphone Part**

www.schott-music.com

Mainz · London · Madrid · New York · Paris · Prague · Tokyo · Toronto

Vibraphone

# Between Sisters

Alvin Singleton (1990)

Rita Dove

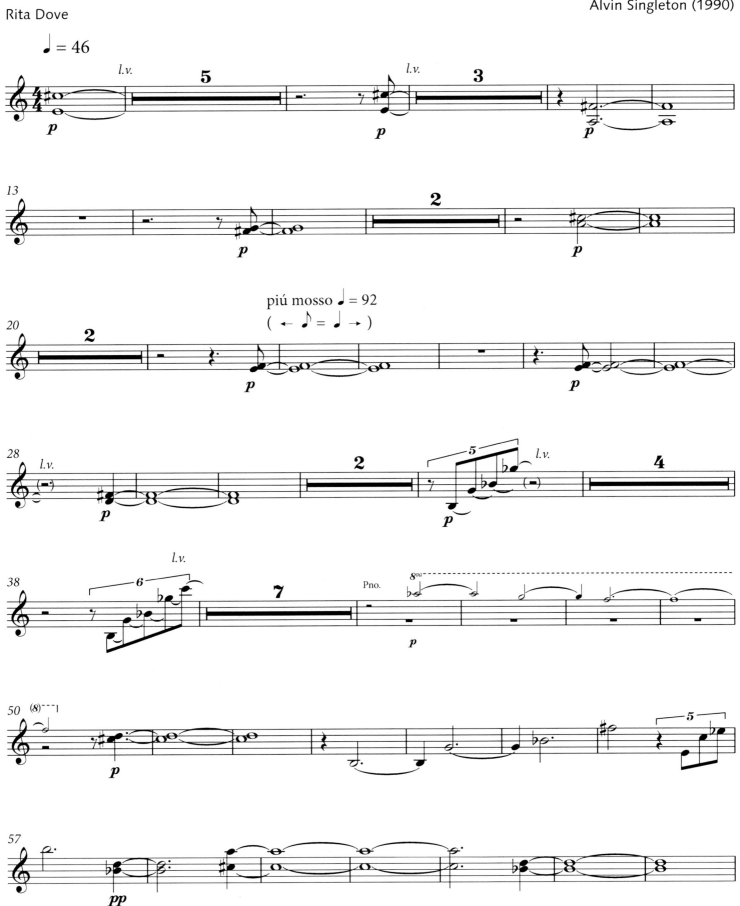

## Vibraphone

meno mosso ♩ = 46

( ← ♪ = ♩ → )

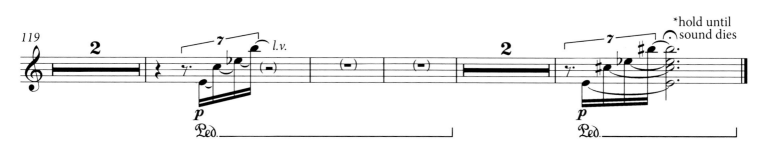

Alvin Singleton

b.1940

# Between Sisters

for Soprano, Alto Flute, Vibraphone, and Piano

**ED 30040**
ISMN 979-0-60001-062-2

**Piano Part**

www.schott-music.com

Mainz · London · Madrid · New York · Paris · Prague · Tokyo · Toronto
© 2010 SCHOTT MUSIC CORPORATION, New York · Printed in USA

Piano

# Between Sisters

Rita Dove

Alvin Singleton (1990)

♩ = 46

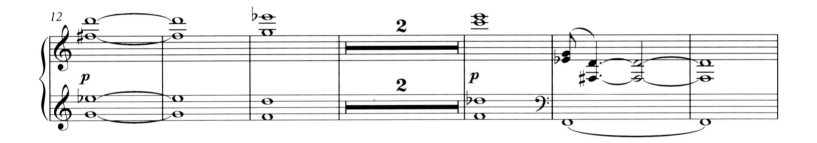

piú mosso ♩ = 92

( ← ♪ = ♩ → )

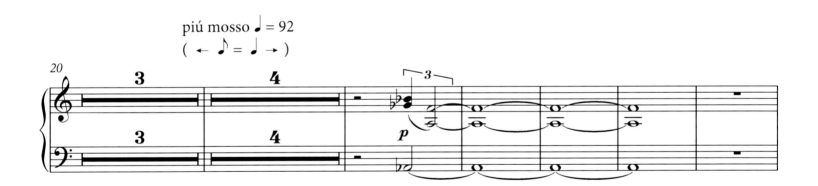

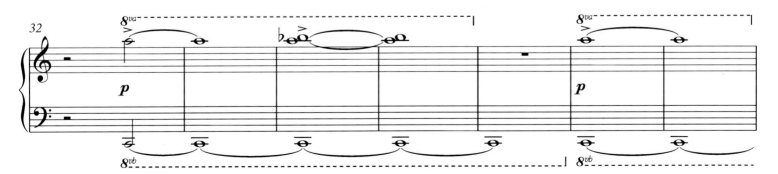

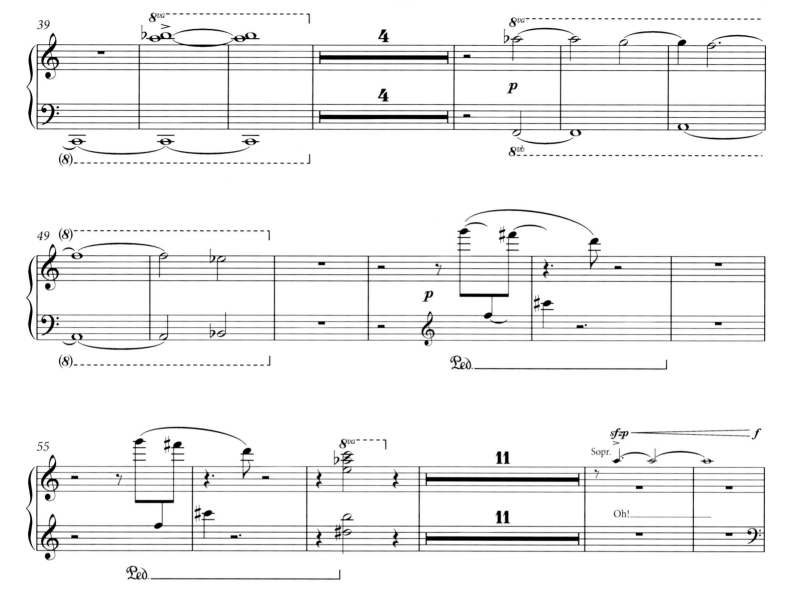

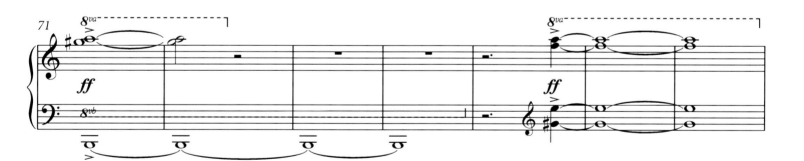

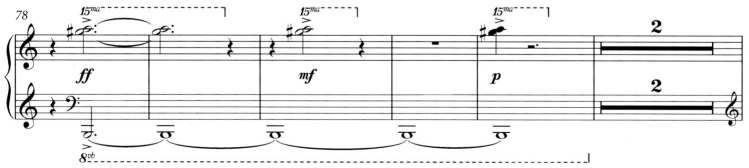

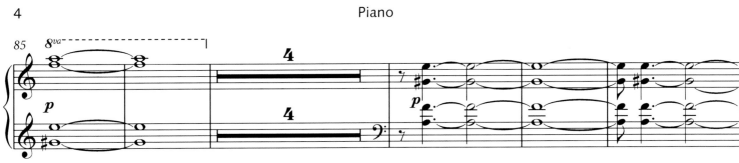

meno mosso ♩ = 46

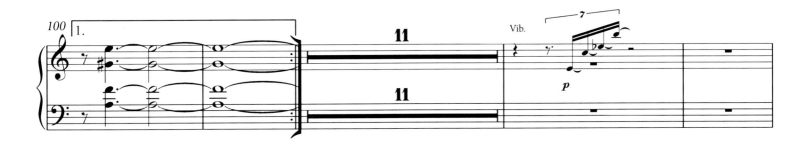

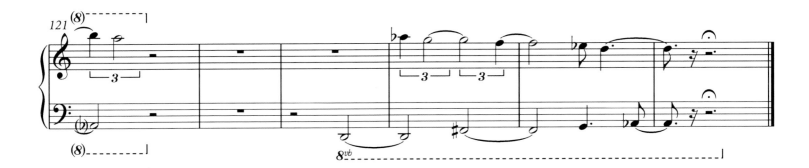

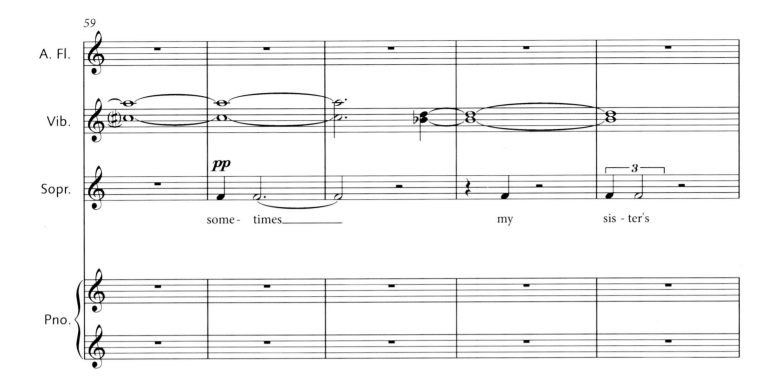

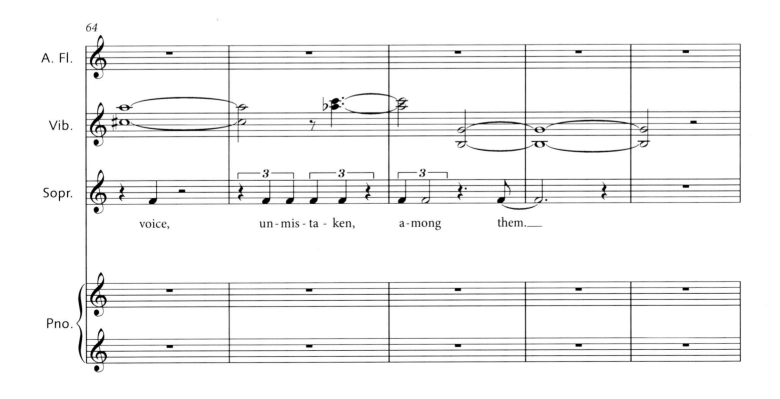

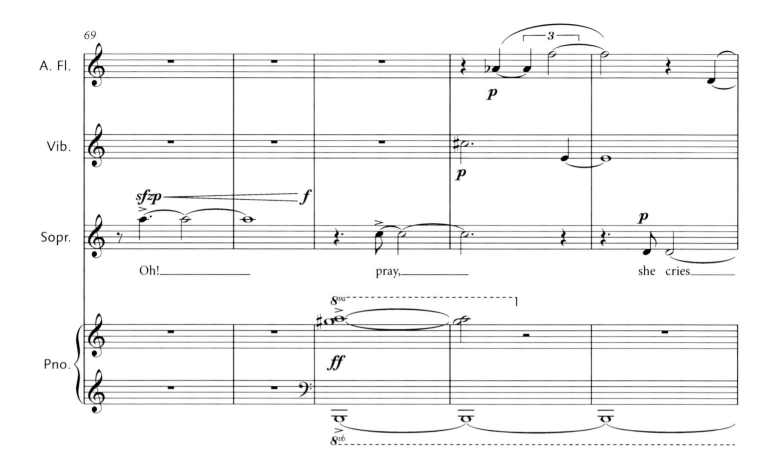

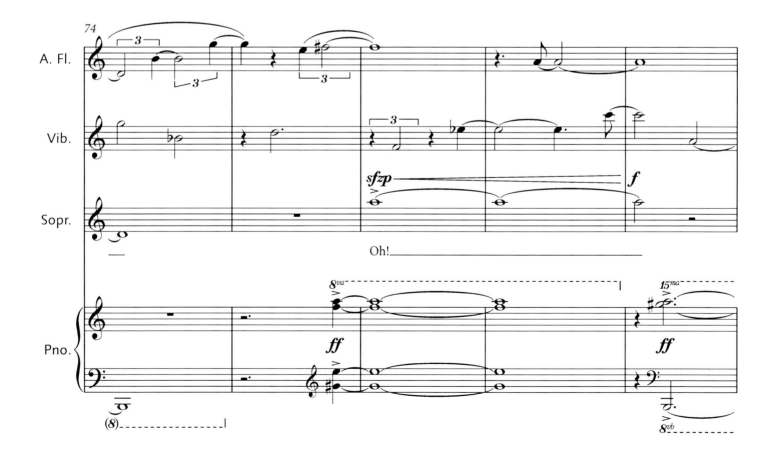

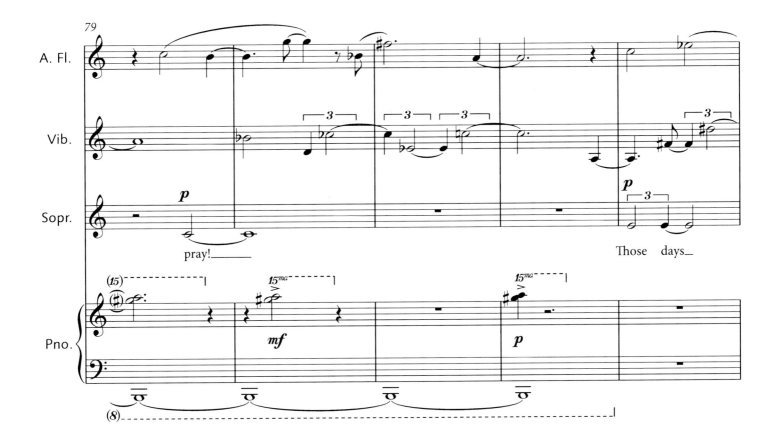

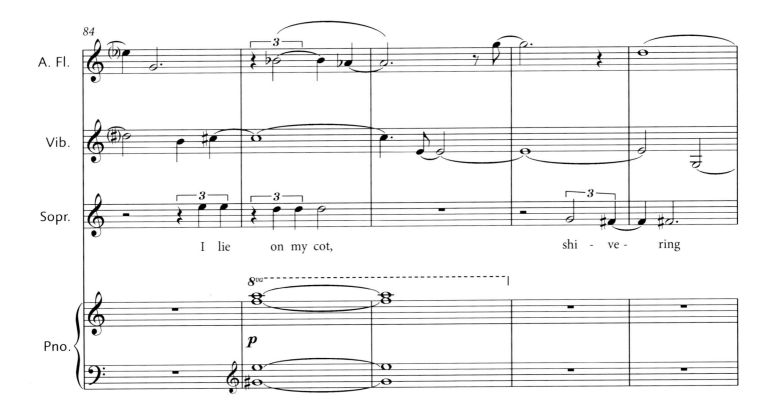

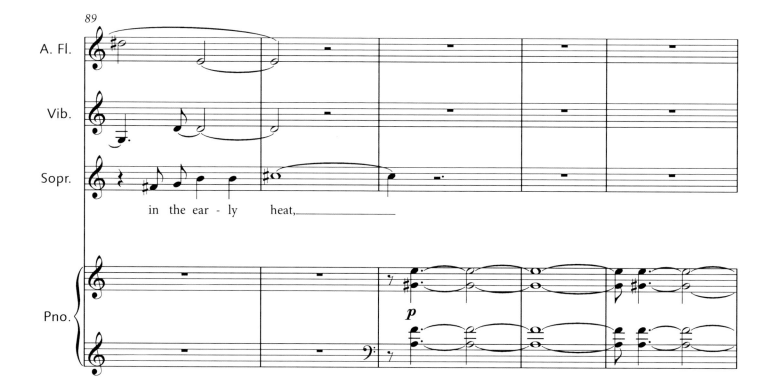

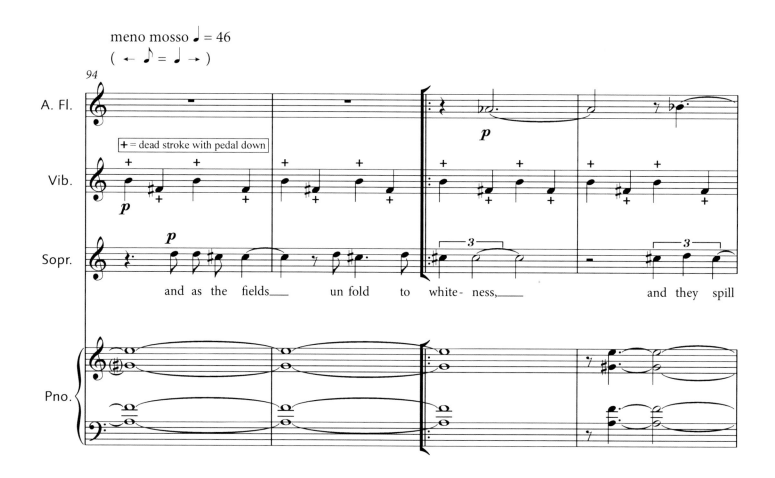

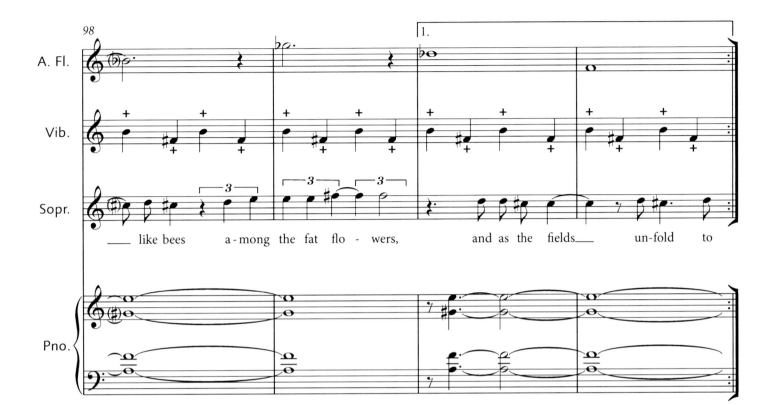

like bees a-mong the fat flo - wers, and as the fields___ un-fold to

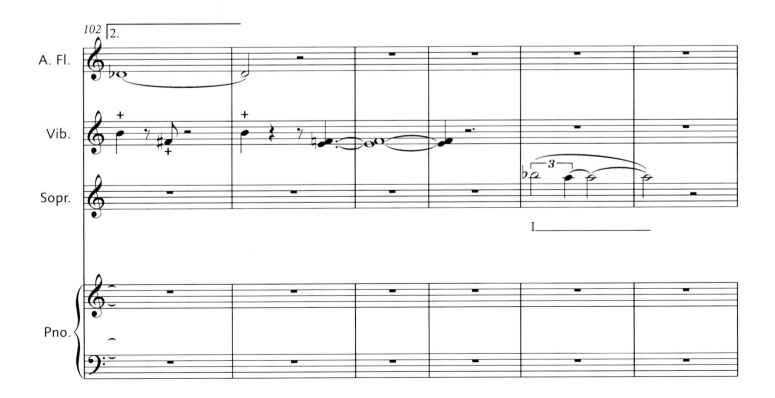

I_____

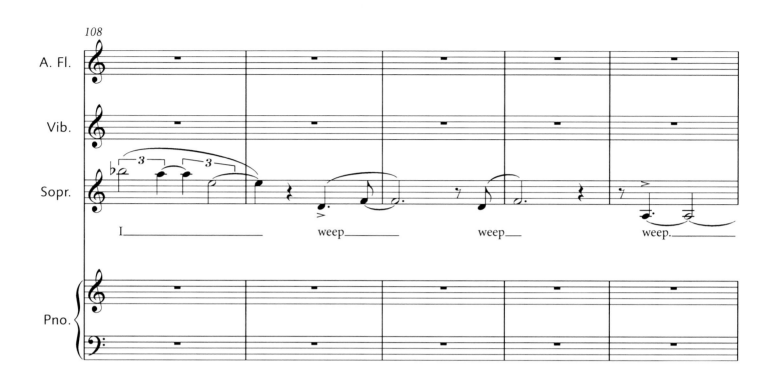

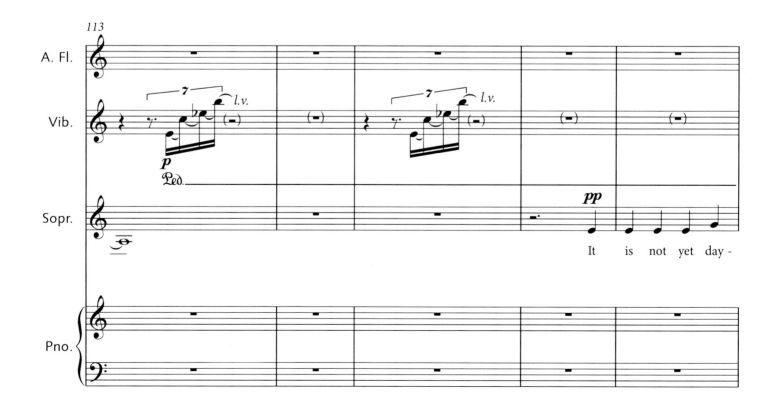

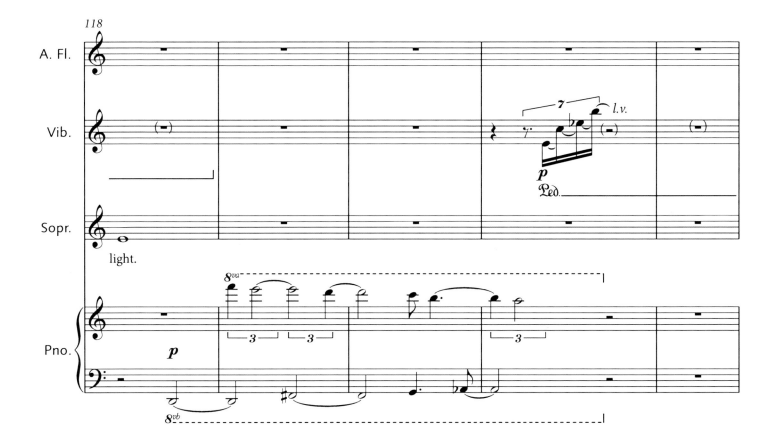

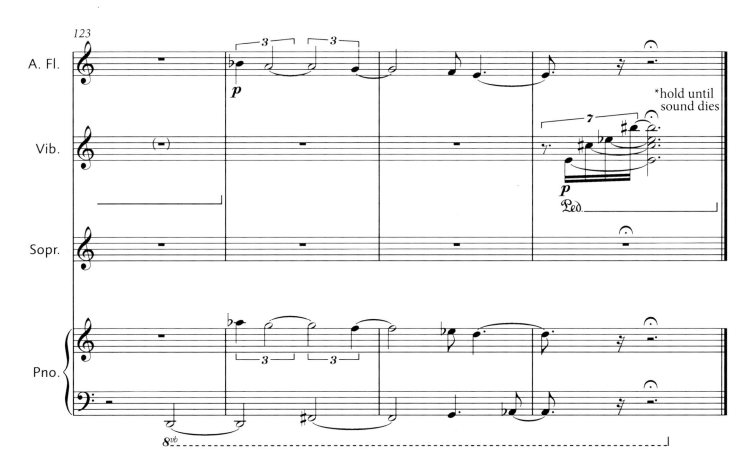

*October 20, 1990*
*Spelman College Atlanta*